# Postage Due
*Poems & Prose Poems*

# Postage Due

## Julie Marie Wade

*Marie Alexander Poetry Series, Volume 17*
*Series Editor: Robert Alexander*
*Editor: Nickole Brown*

WHITE PINE PRESS / BUFFALO, NEW YORK

WHITE PINE PRESS
P.O. Box 236 / BUFFALO, NEW YORK 14201
www.whitepine.org

Edited by Nickole Brown

Publication of this book was made possible, in part, with public funds from
the New York State Council on the Arts, a State Agency.

## ACKNOWLEDGMENTS

I am grateful to the editors of the journals in which many of these poems were previously published, somtimes under different titles: "Advent (Yeager)," *The Tusculum Review*. "(Ambiva)Lent," *Diner*. "Hester Prynne & the Palinode of the Anti-Love" and "Morton's Girl," *Gargoyle Magazine*. "Mr. Clean," *Hiriam Poetry Review*. "For Bridget Wilson, Whose Favorite Word Is/Was Eleemosynary," "For Anna Shope, Who I Always Hated in High School," "Parts of Speech," and "For the Pretty Boy of the Starched White Shirts," *Offcourse Literary Journal*. "Fugue," *Literal Latte*. "Rapture," *Scrivener Creative Review*. "Pentecost" and "The False Mirror," *Front Porch Journal*. "Letter to Judy Garland as Dorothy Gale" and "Letter to Judy Garland as Francis Gumm," *Ghost Ocean Magazine*. "Sometimes Lightning Strikes Twice" and "Bridges (Or a Letter to a Woman I Once Loved)," *Open 24 Hours*. "Thinking of Carl Lull, His Deaf Mother, His Left Hand," *Inscape*. "Epiphany," *Diner*. "Vanna's Dream," *Barrelhouse*.

"Postcard to Mother," published in Fall 2005 by Poetry Jumps Off the Shelf, appeared on java jackets & bookmarks throughout Madison, Wisconsin, as part of a public arts project themed "Postage Due."

Cover image: *The Mayor of Doubt* by Kirsten Deirup. Copyright ©2012 by Kirsten Deirup.
Used by permission of the artist.

First Edition.

ISBN: 978-1-935210-44-3

Printed and bound in the United States of America.

Library of Congress Control Number: 2012948059

*For Angie*
*A love letter—this life with you*

"Some days we wad our papers up
and throw them away.  Some days, some years.
And the ones who come close but do not love us,
cannot love us, I'd say to let them pass through
painlessly, rivers of dust through a window.
They have nothing to do with you."

—Naomi Shihab Nye

# CONTENTS

ADVENT

EPIPHANY

*Men tossing fish at Pike Place Market*
*SEATTLE, WASHINGTON*
*Photo by: Carl Sands*

I wish I had kissed you again—

And harder.

Seattle Souvenir Store - USA

POSTCARD

MANDIE SALAZAR
Mrs. Kolbe's Class
Fifth Grade, 1990

# LENT

"Vagueness is personal!"
—Rae Armantrout

## AUBADE

i.

The moon glowers

in the summer
heat

Trees occlude

the wall of bricks behind them

Ruptured beehives,

cracked open on concrete

Now & then,

a swarm of angry WASPs

*Do you think you'll still love me in 20 years?*

ii.

In Pittsburgh, the men carry heavy lunch boxes;

there is a sadness to their stoop & swagger

I can't believe the paradox: heat rises as light falls—
        uncanny

Pool cue                    Mood light                    Magic eight ball

I remember being born.

To Norfolk—pronounced "Nor-fuck" by the natives

Bite it, spit out the piece
you have bitten, dig
your fingers in &
move around under the skin,
counter-clockwise

Stay close. The earth is shaking.
(or)
I see you,
even when
you're hidden.

# Vertigo (Or A Letter to the Man I Almost Married)

Dear C—
*belated, a little more than 10 years*

(I've heard women in love default to flattery; after love, allegory.)

Here in the future I find I have not much to say to you. It is as if all the while I was loving you, or calling it love, or wanting so much to believe, I was climbing a ladder toward an attic window—rung by rung—the worry of unfulfilled obligation guiding me fist over fist. And what is love if not, at least in part, obligation?

So I kept climbing, despite the rattling & the wind, despite the fact that sometimes you were not even watching or sending down words of encouragement or cups lassoed in rope of water. And at the top when at last I reached it—the ledge, the sill, the Utmost—I made a turn & saw for the first time in aerial dimension the distance I had grown—the devastation possible at such great height.

Then, your hand was stretching out to me, but I didn't want to go in. I could see clearly how the pickets of the gray fences were really spears, & the oak trees, despite their majesty, suffered at the spine, & I remembered something Roosevelt said about fear during the Great Depression & how his wife had urged the embracing of it, not the turning away.

So which did I fear more—loving or not—to be certain & dissatisfied or uncertain & (perhaps) equally so?

And besides all that, white is not my best color. I like something blue or violet maybe—a gentle, fierce, & sordid purity, which is saying something, coming from me.

I could not permit hesitance. I could not afford brevity or lace.
There in the window your face, the chestnut-brown of your boyish curls,
& your thick man-hand, which I had intended, after all, to exonerate.

At that moment, I wanted nothing so much as to leave you, never to see you
again. —To forget what I had (mistakenly) promised.

It was not malice: of this I am certain. It was simply desperation in an
unrealized form:

Desperate, at first, to reach you.
Desperate, at last, to fall away.


My Apology,
(without regret),


J

## (Ambiva) Lent

Waiting to buy books until after Apocalypse, Energy Crisis, Election of an Independent. (Is Nader still running this year?) Unspent dowry: Ten-pack of pencils for 99¢. Good Will chair newly refurbished. Cocktail onions served with—permission to forget. What's your pleasure? Chaucer (or) that soothing feeling as the bath tub faucet passes over your smallest toes.

## Arthur Dimmesdale, Alone in the Closet
## with a Bloody Scourge

I remember when all I wanted was to fuck:
      the urge curdling every cultivated propriety.
I had not so much as sniffed a woman, never tippled in the terrible, tender
places her clothes concealed: damp armpits sprouting with hairs, ankle-bones,
shoulder-bones bewitching.

And the grease of the thighs at the point where they come together—delta of
heat, of fragrant fire.

When she said yes, a soft almost inaudible permission; when she lay back &
spread herself to the place I should enter, it was Satan himself offering to
Christ the temple—whole world in exchange for a prayer.

*If you will only bow down & worship me.*

I felt the Serpent himself attending: tongue piercing groin, dust filling belly,
that hunger that is like no other seizing hold of my (once-iron) will.

In that moment, my eyes opened to the darkest of pleasures, which turned to
the deepest of pains. How she was silent, how complicit / unflinching—how
bold in the face of her sin.

*A woman is a grave,* my father warned me.

I walk dead before God & men.

## Hester Prynne & the Palinode of the Anti-Love

I wonder how it is that men can live with themselves, though it is plain to see women cannot live with them in any salubrious way.

———————————

They come to us, greedy & hungry, & when we feed them—sparing little (if any) for ourselves—they resort to scorn, punishment for the passion we cannot sustain.

———————————

There is a man I've known, whose name I must not reveal. He expects our souls shall burn in Hell for remittance of our Sin.

———————————

He is a True Believer.

———————————

But a woman's soul burns in Hell already upon this rank, dark earth, & men have never understood or offered solace from her plight.

———————————

From my Sin, a small reprieve from loneliness, though God has cursed me doubly with the absence of a son.

———————

"Daughter," I tell this restless child. "It is treachery to live as woman in this world. Cherish your youth with its blessed androgyny—to move loosely between the skirts of women & the shoulders of men.

———————

Be warned: at first blood, they will smell you, anticipate the stain, & before you have even washed yourself clean, descend upon you—vicious, blood-thirsty dogs."

Resin Door, 1993; The Mattress Factory
Pittsburgh, Pennsylvania
Photo by: Virginia Russell

Thank you for the birthday present,
Mrs. Pittman. I know I was only four
and should have thanked you more
properly at the time instead of cling-
ing shyly to the back of my grand-
mother's legs. I know you felt it was
your place to tell my mother how
ungrateful I was. Now, Mrs. Pittman,
I feel it is my place to tell you—
she already knew.

North Side Art Show - PA

### POSTCARD

Mrs. Ann Pittman
c/o Fauntlee Hills

w. the manicured lawn, the
manicured husband, and all
the manicured children who
have long since moved away.

## For Bridget Wilson, Whose Favorite Word Is/Was Eleemosynary

We failed Chemistry together. A series of one-act plays. *Glitter, Arugula,* & *Cribbage.* Her hair "coarse as a horse," & yellow like straw. Not pretty but— Not pretty but—Little braids in the bang-line. A kerchief choking it back.

And I thought, there must be something special about a girl so easily mistaken for a sunflower. In Southern France—she was with her whole family, & they all looked like sunflowers, standing there in the high grass.

If I could have found the words then—*clarinet, cacophony*—if I could have found the words—then, I would have thanked her for teaching me about t-shirts tugged over long sleeves in winter & blue jeans shredded at the seams. And gritty, Guthrie-laced sneakers: hours of mad cartoons.

Oh, Bridget, what we don't learn over tepid cafeteria food! What the ACRONYMS can't begin to describe. I wanted to bury my face in your hair so many times, stretched out on your binder, bulky & blue, studded with white-out stars.

Always, a reasonable distance—yet *Flux.*      *Sestina.*      *Yarn.*

When you were gone, the storms quieted. I got on with my studies. *Calculus. Calligraphy.* My future set out like a dinner plate, yours an imponderable meal.

# For Anna Shope, Who I Always Hated in High School

"Shope, Shope, Is-o-tope, skinny knock-knees jumping rope, father's dead & mother's broke, bet she's back to smokin' dope…"

It was wrong, Anna, & I'm sorry. You never knew what I thought about you, the twisted rhymes I turned over in my mind. Or how I begrudged you that confidence erupting out of your eyes, shooting up from your fingers, frenetically raised, catapulting you across the classroom.

I wish I could call it jealousy, & be done: admit that I wanted your grades in Geometry, your fearlessness in the face of A.P. Physics. The ambidextrous brain that balanced itself with perfect book-end scores—the Verbal & the Quantitative questions.

When I look back, I see my voyeurism & your face, a place for only one of us in those hard-wood halls. And your father, who had died of AIDS, whose death you mourned so openly I shuddered.

Attention, I thought, was all you craved.

Then again at Tolo with the nameless boys, I danced in circles pending your arrival. How to say this—that I studied you in high school as much as any of my subjects: the ellipsis of your speech, the emphatic curl of your lip when you were certain you had found the answer. And perhaps you had.

That night at the Aquarium in the pretty blue room, when I told my date I was searching for the loo… I found you instead with some eager young man's hands spread tight across your stomach in the pretty blue dress.

There were sharks swimming overhead, & the skylights cast finned shadows on the floor, & your mouth was open on his, fluttering like a bird determined to bury itself, & a dizzy heat rose up in me so hard & fast I had to lean against the wall to keep from falling.

We both graduated with 4.0s. You went pre-med, & I became an English major.

*Are you a doctor yet? Am I poet?*

I'm not sure how the measure's made, but I feel sure you'll make it. And as for me & my weak knees: I've been kissed that way I once could only dream.

PARTS OF SPEECH

*Cantaloupe*: serendipitous selection; deep green of the vigorous rind

*Salutation*: coming or going, a wave is always the same

*Curfew*: I want you home with me, in bed

*Helix, Entendre,* & all things folded in half

*Television*: if you look hard enough, there's a mirror inside

*Circumcision,* & other pilferings of the Body

*Polygon*: encompassing an indeterminate number of sides

*Sunrise*: conversation piece & practical light

*Euphemism*—the one they forgot—the reason for two chairs at this table

# FUGUE

At the last minute, the pilot light blows out:
"come out, come out, wherever you are"
my tussle with synecdoche & stars


Ubiquitous, as Dalí's mustache
a page-turner, pot-stirrer
epidemic of asphalt
salt


"Come out, come out, wherever you are"
I hadn't realized that I was hiding


Twelfth-grade theology class:
Contemporary Problems
Jack Cassidy & Shirley Jones
I never understood about annulment—


And the backlash of theodicy
in the Catholic schools:
Voltaire's *Candide* by now a classic


"Come out, come out, wherever you are"
fissure in the two-party system:
Why this again, the white or wheat?
where sourdough? where pumpernickel? rye?

Silhouettes & suffragettes
we pantomime confusion with Winkin', Blinkin', & Nod
I seem to remember—


My mother, & what if
she had fallen the way I have: for a schoolgirl
in a whirlwind romance? They might have stepped out
(the plank of reason like a diving board),


sprung high, & closing their eyes,
the shark-face in the water
shattering to shards of glass


"Come out, come out, wherever you are,"
& the counting, & the curtsies, & the new-fangled whiplash—
I was trying to be a dancer
in the pink-&-white-striped leotard, but more like a stoic flamingo


or Ostrich with Head in Sand. . .
which—if you didn't know—
is also a glass, is also primed to be shattered


The PBS special said "come out, come out,
wherever you are," & ostriches were mating in the ribald heat—
females, engorged with blood, & screeching

I seem to remember—
those "hand-painted dream photographs," no science
less precise than preservation...
"Come out, come out, wherever you are"


*Will the real inkblot please stand up?*
Painting myself in the corner of these poems
a quiet flaw in form you'd hardly notice


the button collection & the postcard homage
& Tampax coarse as cattails in the Bathhouse basement—
Bathhouse, *the theatre*, that is


I have to watch myself when I'm giving away too much,
coaxing the small snail out of its shell—
"come out, come out, wherever you are"—
when I'm ever-so-slightly shy


Parapraxes & polemics
& the wood-cutting class: I'd like a cool scythe
to slice
this Spanish moss in half

Moony-eyed for Melville's
"damp November of the soul," & the teacher
with her desk barraged by apples:


*Put the speculum down, step away from the body*
Or flinching at the brush of my mother's handi-crafts


"You'll be the life of the party"
If you would just come out, come out,
wherever you are—
the rainbow caravan's departing.


But I can't breathe here, despite the bridegroom in his Baptist best:
*Could you draw me a parallelogram?*

In the bleachers, in the nosebleeds,
sneakers without laces:
Velcro, & aluminum-free anti-perspirant, & Robitussin straight from the
bottle

Because Sandy, the ballerina, was so beautiful—
And the ice cubes were artificial in the plastic glass: little fruit-shapes frozen
by science to last—

"Come out, come out, wherever you are"
the loudspeaker booms
at the Miss Pre-Teen America pageant


Christina Shoemaker took home the crown, &
the runners-up got to meet Clinton


If I could only stop shuffling my feet
Acolyte, fidgeting—the static
on the phone every Fourth of July,
wishing a happy birthday


What we regret about Ouija boards, Tinkerbell, & Canadian Geese:
how they never come out wherever they are,
& always seem to speak another language

# Rapture

I haven't had zucchini bread since Lynette Smith's house in the summer of 1984—or was it '85? I remember she had two sons, Brian & Russell, & her husband planned to leave them each a million dollars when he died. Lynette wasn't interested so much in the money, but in baking with berries fresh from her garden, shuffling plums into baskets & letting them stew all afternoon in an elegant, silver strainer. Len drove a station wagon the size of a train, so when fast travelers attempted to tailgate, he slammed on the brakes & let them slam right into him. Never got hurt. Laughed all the way home. "Another dent, another dollar," he always said. But Lynette laid out in the half-shade, half-sun of the sprawling backyard with her hair pulled back in a purple bandana, reading *The Thornbirds* & waiting for the bread to rise. And I thought, even at my young age—*A woman is a rapturous thing.*

# PENTECOST

"You have no faith in your own language.
So you invest
authority in signs
you cannot read with any accuracy."
                                    —Louise Glück

# PENTECOST

Or the first time, smoking, hairs raised
all over your body. A second drag to similar effect.

Now a dark man lingers in the alley
of the dream, dressed in your father's bathrobe.

1987 is a bad year to ask questions.

Cut to: You're not sure if the hole in your body
is an outlet or an inlet. When a man plugs into you,
you disconnect.

[Which is not to say anything specific about sexual politics.
Which is not to imply any inherent distrust of the opposite sex.]

*Diet or Regular?*

Your mother prefers large women for friends.
Lessens the competition.

1992 is a very bad year to ask questions.

Soon after, your dead grandmother's ring disappears.
A cousin suspects you. After all, yours was the prettiest stone.

In the Straits of Juan de Fuca, you shower for an audience
& feel your flesh dissolve.

*Get Smart* is the only good show on television.

[Which is not to say anything specific about Nostalgia.
Which is not to imply any inherent distrust of Progress.]

Rob Hildebrant at the beach—it is almost
beautiful. You eat licorice & fortune cookies
to excess; he takes you for a ride in his skiff.

*Whatever happened to the fish-tail braid?*
*When did it fall out of fashion?*

For the rest of your life then, you're making sense of, just trying to make
sense of:

TRESPASSING SIGNS

WANTED POSTERS

By 1994, you have run out of questions.
You write stories in the omniscient third.

Lamarck's theory: Inheritance of Acquired Characteristics.

*Can they pass it onto you? Will you catch it?*

Pauline Gates propositions you, leans on your locker,
writes love notes.

1997: brief resurgence of questions & a survey of horror films.

"Camp" enters your vocabulary with a vengeance.

Meanwhile, your other grandmother
falls in love with Alex Trebek.
In time, you forgive her.
(She's half-Canadian.)

Cut

In the new millennium, life turns
abysmal: 4 months in London, & still you couldn't get laid.

Your flatmate believes you have a crush on her.

You wish you had a crush on Someone.

Graduation: a long walk in hot sun. A vow:
No more nylon socks. Even on special occasions.

You accuse your mother
of failing
to love you

[Which is not to say you didn't want her to.
Which is not to say you did.]

Mistaken for a Christian for the

last time—

A Necessary Hair Cut

In the kitchen, admiring: Anna suggests you look like a lesbian.

*What does a lesbian look like again?*

2002: To Hell with Questions

You sleep with your friend & refuse to wake up.

Cut to: *The Cabinet of Dr. Caligari.*
Final presentation
for "Word, Image, Art."

Long overdue, you consider
the implications of
the Side Note:

[as a child, you used to play
maracas. you used to shake
a tambourine. how, now—
this sudden
fear of noises?]

"I want the opposite of *Cheers.*
A place where no one knows my name."

That can be arranged.

But—before the lights come up—

*Are there any questions?*

Private Prairie, 1991; The Mattress Factory
Pittsburgh, Pennsylvania
Photo by: Winnifred Lutz

New Commandmants:

Thou shalt love thy lover's body.

Thy shalt fuck they lover's brains out.

Thou shalf not be ashamed of
        thy cunt nor thy heart.

North Side Art Show - PA

POSTCARD

Pastor Gary Jensen

St. Paul's of Shorewood
Lutheran Church

What I couldn't have said
then

## Letter to Judy Garland as Dorothy Gale

"There are a good many roads here," observed the shaggy man, turning slowly around, like a human windmill. "Seems to me a person could go 'most anywhere, if starting from a place like this."

Each time, crossing Kansas, I think of you there, among the baleful hay of Wamego.

One Halloween, in a blue gingham dress with braids in my hair & a fat cat crammed in a basket, I set out down the dustless streets, determined to make my adventure.

It's not that I cared less, you see; it's not that I've ever forgotten. But there's something in the air that can't quite contain you, in the faces of family & farmhands you once thought you knew. (They thought they knew you, too.)

Dorothy, I'm wishing I could show you how the longing just stops—or suddenly fades—while Aunt Em in the crystal grows fainter.

Perhaps I've lost my good heart like the Tin Man, leaning here with this ax in my hand. Still, don't you reckon—every now & again—a cyclone could really come in handy?

We have planes, trains, & automobiles. We even have hot air balloons. But, Dorothy, a word about those ruby shoes: if they're really yours, as they were never mine:

Close your eyes, by all means; click your heels three times. There's no place like—no place like—

Say Helena. Say Galveston. Say Kalamazoo. Just promise you won't say Home.

## Letter to Judy Garland as Francis Gumm

You didn't imagine—how could you?—the fame the future had in store. Days like these I half-expect to see your face on a pro-life poster, testament to the talent & beauty of the unwanted child.

You were the baby, the one who came late & lonely & never longed for. (I was the first, the last, the only: nothing but a promised victory in a lengthy war.)

I remember the sound of you singing in the dark, my Fisher-Price record player that spun the past softly, made it stick. Spun the past so sweetly, in fact, I mistook it for the present, & you for the dreamed-of sister, warbling in the other room.

When I saw you the first time on our black-&-white TV set—grown but still small, a pretty Midwestern girl making believe she was Hollywood in the strange disembodiment of the stage—

Your voice a tower dwarfing your form, shrinking the world to one raw desire: hit the high note, hit it every time, & there was lift-off in your language & the dark flutter of your eyes—your lungs a cannon you were blasting out of...

It was Judy you became, mid-air, over the rainbow & over the moon; Judy, brought low again under the big tent—all eyes on her; the spotlight too bright, the encore too long—

Judy, the great hush like snow that has fallen.
Francis, the name buried under the snow.

What I know about Sister Janice amounts to a heap of old notebook paper headed for the shredder. But I studied her for a while, in high school, during keyboarding class & calligraphy.

She was perfectly ambidextrous (well, she taught herself to be), & sometimes after school in the art room I'd see her sketching, both hands simultaneously, a portrait per page.

I know she talked less about Jesus than any nun I had ever known—& I have known a lot of nuns. Plethora. Myriad. Any trumped-up word for a team o' plenty, & I guarantee I've known that many nuns & then some.

But they don't like to be called "nuns" anymore, which sounds like none, like nothing, as if they didn't exist because they didn't have sex or drive cars or deviate from a fixed monastic budget of approximately $85 a month.

And that was another curious fact about Sister Janice: she did drive a car, & she never seemed cross the way the others did, as if celibacy had finally gotten the better of her. Beat her down.

She didn't walk like a nun, talk like a nun, & she sure as holy mary mother of god didn't dress like a nun. Sister Janice was different. For starters, she was Dominican, which the Sisters of the Holy Names of Jesus & Mary seemed to regard as somewhat... laissez-faire.

She drove a car, as I mentioned, & probably has a cell phone by now, & her hair was never only blunt-cut, let alone shaved off bald. She liked especially Hawaiian shirts, which she wore with alternating peach & pink pants, & in the springtime, khaki shorts with white knee-high socks & orthopedic shoes.

Sister Janice seemed to me like a sister without any sisters. An only child. The freak at the family reunion. She came late to mass & sat in back & sometimes she even looked bored.

Last I heard she had left Holy Names, packed up her easel & coloring books, a real live nun-on-the-run. And I thought then how I rather missed her, just knowing she was gone, & how she had always been to me less "nun" than "sister," & how I had heard one other thing about her worthy to repeat:

That already, in her life thus far, she'd been struck by lightning twice—ecstatic, illuminated, a nun on fire—those late nights without rosary, walking to her car.

Artist: Yves Tanguy
1927, 92 x 65 cm, Oil on Canvas
Museum of Modern Art, New York


Perhaps it is war-time, & Riding Hood has been besieged by birds.
I cannot promise you anything but doves.
Like those scattering the walkways in Honolulu.
Or gold pelicans skirting the long Orlando highway.


A lightning-bolt strikes under your cursor.
Smoke from a chimney that hasn't felt fire in years.
What to make of the inquiry now, the insinuation?
A kettle teeming with kippers & other assorted fish.


Slow gradient of gray, ascending.
The unkempt woman ragged in the wind.
Pastiche is just a softer word for paranoia.
The Wolf acquires another county seat.

# For the Pretty Boy of the Starched White Shirts

I would have done anything for you.
Do you understand?
Anything.

It was desperate, & I am not proud
of the fact that all my feminisms
fell right out the window in immaculate defenestration
the first time your eye lingered on mine under the auspices of
our "meeting of the minds."

That is, I wanted to unbutton each proper button
of your starched white shirt &
let my hands loose under your Hanes classic cotton crew,
which I was almost absolutely certain that you wore.

You said "coordinate," & I was baited like a guppy on your line.
A book you passed across the table,
& I touched it as a relic from a foreign land.

You said "historicize," & I could think only of zippers missing teeth.
Your body bare beneath the sheets. My legs split. My lamp lit.
Caroling, we'd say, in time for Christmas.

What love letters could I have written but hagiography?
What kisses could I have given but my whole breath bent beyond
asphyxiation?

And the fantasy—I'm not too shy to say—
of being stung by a Portuguese man-of-war, entangled in its ten-foot

tentacles, while you naked, unmoored in the Mediterranean,
having ventured away from the elegant catamaran that brought you lonely

to these shores, pulled me free & weak & weightless in the water,
guiding me over gentle waves toward an uninhabited enclave
where we would turn *From Here to Eternity*

in the mood light moonlight,
tongues swollen from traipsing the length of our skins,
& over white wine & oysters on your decadent yacht,

suggest how we really ought to get away like this more often.

# THE NOTE

Everyone always thought I was a Good Girl. Teachers especially. Good girl, good grades, good manners. My mother knew otherwise but was content to let them believe the lie. Oh yes, she'd smile, such a delightful child. But underneath that pretty, painted hide, I could hear her growling.

Once, in fifth grade, Mrs. Kolbe sent me downstairs to the Principal's office. She had a note she needed signed—one piece of white paper folded in half & slipped in an unlicked envelope. And I could speculate what was written on that page had something to do with Shawn Michelsen who sat next to me & always shoved his hands a little too deep in his pockets, kept them there through all of Language Arts & most of Science.

What I should have done, I'll tell you now, I should have opened it, read for myself the contents of the teacher's controlled & nuanced pen, tucked it back in the envelope like a Barbie doll to bed. If I had—such a simple act, alone in the stairwell with no one watching—this would be a poem about transgression & not regret; a poem about the courage we find, in small ways, to change ourselves.

Shawn Michelsen & what became of his dusty blond head, & his teeth begging for braces, & the warm, temporal bliss of the body that can give so much & feel so good when we are permitted, at last, to indulge. In his future: a fall from monkey bars that nearly breaks a rib; his mother's cancer eating away her skin; & the one time at the Christmas party when he reached over, drew out his hand, & placed it ever so cautiously on my partly exposed knee. Perhaps I wish also I hadn't brushed him away, hadn't turned abruptly fearing that someone would see.

Everyone always thought I was a Good Girl. Except my mother.

When I got acne, she said, "It's the meanness coming out of you" & squeezed her tweezers. She wasn't fooled by double dimples & a pleated skirt. She told me I could schmooze anyone for a while. But then the nuns began to distrust my dialect of doubt & eulogize. And the paper against annulment took a hit of hard-won red lines.

"Are you trying to ruin everything?" my mother cried. "Don't you know a thing like this could keep you out of college!"

Just this morning, in my eighth collegiate year, my third degree, I sat down & wrote a note. For Mrs. Kolbe & Sister Mary Annette & for my mother, who would not open it even if it came on daisy-yellow stationery with calligraphy spelling out her name.

"I am tired of pretending," the note said.

And as for Shawn Michelsen—who learned how to love himself far better than I did—this poem: about Good Girls & what we remember on rainy, Pittsburgh mornings with our hands shoved a little too deep in our pockets.

## My Mother Attempts to Procure Me a Prom Date through the JCPenney Catalog

Dear Stafford Shirt Man,

You are such a handsome, clean-cut fellow! I always marvel at your impeccable style & all-American good looks each time I pass the dress shirt display at the Southcenter JCPenney's. I always say I'm going to write you a letter, but then somehow time gets away from me—a mother's work is never done!—& another week goes by before I think of it again.

Anyway, I'm not writing on behalf of myself. (I've been a happily married woman for 28 years.) I'm actually writing on behalf of my daughter. She's only sixteen but quite mature for her age—& very, very accomplished. She has played piano for eight years & taken ballet, tap, & jazz for twelve. She also makes straight As in school & is a varsity runner for the Holy Names cross-country team. We just couldn't be more proud of her.

I have to tell you, though. Being such a smart, capable young woman hasn't always worked in Julie's favor. She doesn't have much time for extra-curricular socializing, & being that we have made the sacrifice to send her to an all-girls (quite exclusive) Catholic preparatory school, she doesn't meet very many boys. And the boys she does meet, even if they are roughly her age—well, she's already past them intellectually.

All my husband & I have ever wanted for our beautiful only child is the kind of happiness she has worked for & deserves. She's too busy & shy to ask any of the boys she knows to her junior prom—coming up in May of this year—so I was wondering if you might be available to escort our Julie to the dance. Of course we'd love to have you over to our place for dinner first, & Bill (my husband) wouldn't mind at all driving you to & from the dance, which is scheduled to be held at the Daughters of the American Revolution

Mansion at the far end of Broadway on Capitol Hill.

I don't know how busy your modeling schedule is these days, though it's plain to see that you are in <u>high</u> demand. I would just love to surprise my daughter with the most perfect date for her prom, & for her to show up on the arm of such a perfect gentleman would do wonders for her self-esteem. Not that she's not confident, you understand; just that, with all her accolades, she might seem a bit intimidating to a less accomplished man.

Thank you so much for considering this request. Attached is a picture of Julie & me, taken at the Mother-Daughter Tea. I know you'll agree—she <u>really</u> is a beautiful girl. And the best part is, she's as beautiful on the inside as she is on the outside. I hope you two have a chance to meet!

Sincerely,


Linda M. Wade
March 12, 1996

# Triptych

I.

46 Bonnie Meadow Road
New Rochelle New York

November 3 1991

Dear Mrs. Laura Petrie

You can't imagine what it means to me that we are meeting now in syndication. I am a seventh-grade honor student at Calvary Lutheran School in West Seattle. When I grow up I want to be a writer an oral surgeon & a private investigator like Paul Drake on the <u>Perry Mason</u> series (also in syndication). Do you know him by the way or Della or Perry? They're black-&-white like you but from L.A.

I would also like to be a wife & mother.

You do it so well—always with Capri pants & a smile. And when you get mad it isn't like my mother's mad. It's like a tunnel with a light & the anger's just a train that's passing through.

I think I'd like to <u>be</u> you. I have big white teeth from my father's side of the family but my skin is a bit of a problem. Not perfect for pictures. In fact nowhere near close.

But did I tell you I'm on the cheer team? We're such a small school they don't even hold auditions. Every girl is automatically enrolled. I'm no great cheerleader & no great dancer either nothing like you in the USO show before you found & fell in love with Rob Petrie. And I wonder what that's like because I haven't been in love yet though I did see <u>Barefoot in the Park</u> performed last Christmas.

The fact is though despite skipping sixth grade & not even (yet) shaving my legs I've already had one boyfriend. My mother says I'm too young to have had my heart broken but she's not enlightened like you Laura Petrie. Nowhere near close.

Lee Bennett & I were "hot & heavy" for about a year but then he met Marissa Sheldon. She's no Millie Helper I'll tell you that but I did wish that she had been my friend. She was the prettiest most popular girl in the whole school & I couldn't keep Lee from losing interest in me.

So how do you make it work—love I mean—& how do you keep thin after having kids & do you ever wish you had a job outside the home?

I'm also writing with a practical question even though I tend to get philosophical from time to time & am currently not using commas.

See an anonymous person entered a picture of me (pre-acne) & a statement about my so-far accomplishments (tap jazz ballet piano choir track swimming spelling bee champ six years running & now cheer) in the Miss Pre-Teen America Pageant preliminaries. I have a chance to compete: make a speech wear a prom dress in front of an audience answer questions from judges & perform a talent. My mother thinks a piano solo of Beethoven's "Für Elise" would please the crowd.

But please Laura Petrie what do <u>you</u> think? I'm afraid of losing & afraid of winning. Does that make sense? On the one hand I just want to meet a nice man & be ten years older so I can skip adolescence altogether & go directly to a home of my own. Be something to somebody who will see me in my pajamas & not laugh. We probably won't even sleep in separate beds. But if I become a hit on the pageant circuit then what? A lot of dating & parties & I won't know what to wear…

I just want it all to be over & done with: a husband who trips over the ottoman & a little boy I don't have to see too much.

Please write when you can.

Sincerely


Julie Marie Wade
Fauntlee Hills
(The Water-View Side)

2.

119 North Weatherly
Minneapolis, Minnesota

October 19, 1994

Dear Ms. Mary Richards,

I am choosing the prefix "Ms." instead of the more traditional "Miss" because I know you are a classy & progressive kind of woman. Allow me first to introduce myself. My name is Julie Wade, & I am a first-term sophomore at Holy Names Academy—a Catholic school, even though my parents are Protestant. (I know you're Presbyterian; they're Lutheran.)

To tell the truth, I am quite unsatisfied with my life thus far, & at 15 now, I'm not sure what to expect from the future. I don't have a lot of friends at school. I'm not the kind of high school girl you were. Once, a long time ago, I was in a beauty pageant, & I didn't even make the semi-finals. I used to be better at math, but I'm only pulling a B in Honors Geometry at the moment, & my mom is really fit to be tied. If I do all the extra credit, though, I should be able to eke out an A for my final grade.

I don't know what kind of student you were. My guess is probably average. Not that you aren't really smart, but Roseberg High doesn't sound like it was all that demanding. In the old days, average was OK. It was <u>average</u>. Today the "average" GPA at my high school is 3.6. Excellence used to be oatmeal, & now it's eggs benedict.

But—I'm really not writing to complain. I'm writing to find out a little more about "making it on your own" & how it's done. Do you ever get scared at night, all alone in your own apartment? My friend April & I—she's kind of like my Rhoda—are planning to move in together after college when we go to live in the city. (Our addresses say Seattle, but we don't actually live there. It's just a trick the postal service likes to play.)

So here's the thing: you always say that you want to get married, but you've turned down at least 3 proposals that I can recall. If I had even one guy offer to marry me—as long as he wasn't in prison (or likely to be)—I'd accept that proposal in a hurry. I have a hard time picturing married life, & you seem to be having a fine time without one. And look at Rhoda—she got divorced. Who's to say that couldn't happen to you, too?

So are you playing the field or what? Are you still looking for Mr. Right? Do you ever feel like there might be something wrong with you (not that there is) for being single so long?

I have an aunt—we call her "Lindabird"—& she's at least your age & probably older. She's not as pretty, but I like her clothes, & so far she's basically kept her figure. She wanted to get married & have kids, but my mom says she's close to menopause & it's a shame. Aunt Lindabird hasn't even had sex yet because she thinks it should be saved, but I'm not sure you can have it after 50.

Which brings me to another question, Mary Richards, which I think I can trust you to answer. I'm a bright girl. I can read between the lines of your dialogue—what the censors will (& will not) allow. But you've had sex, haven't you? You're not waiting. You even lived with a man who was training to be a doctor.

I'd like to know how you knew when you were ready to—& if you were even a little bit afraid God might strike you down. I'm around celibacy all day long, & it's starting to be kind of a drag. I still want to be a writer & maybe a counselor. I was thinking maybe I could work with teenagers who need to get laid & get out of religion.

Because frankly, I feel my religion is holding me back, & I notice you don't even go to church at all. Is that because you don't believe in God, or just because you don't believe in the kind of people who believe in God?

There are some nuns here who've got it in for me pretty bad. I'm a good student, but I think annulment's crap, & I've essentially stopped taking communion on the grounds that if transubstantiation is actually real, then we're all a bunch of cannibals & that can't be good for your soul.

Pretty much I'm conflicted because I think I could like being single & having sex with different people—<u>men</u>—& the rest of the time just hanging out with my friends. My parents are Republicans, but once I get to college, I'm joining the Young Democrats. I know you & Phyllis & Rhoda all belong.

I guess I should be wrapping things up because you've had a long day in the newsroom & I have homework to do. More proofs. I hate them. I'm not that certain of anything, & I don't see why we should accept these theorems at face value. (Probably why I'm not on the fast track to earning an A, & Miss Benedict is a stickler for accuracy.)

Mary Richards, did you ever do anything in your whole good & pretty life that you felt ashamed of?

See, I sit next to this girl in Psychology class—Sara—& she's kind of worldly & agnostic & all that, & she's also dating another girl—Heather—at school. And once, I don't know why, but I told Sara Timmons how I kissed Mandie Salazar in fifth grade, even though I already had a boyfriend. She said that probably meant I was a lesbian & the next step was coming out of the closet. But I once had a babysitter named Deanna who had a friend named Heidi, & they got caught making out in a closet with both their shirts off by Deanna's dad. (Sorry if this is too much information.) But by rights then, by Sara's theorem, Deanna had to become a lesbian. Instead, just last year, she married a doctor, & my mother said, "She's set for the rest of her life."

So I guess I wondered if you had ever kissed a girl, or thought about kissing a girl—maybe even a friend—maybe even Rhoda. And if you ever thought (or worried even) that it might make you into a lesbian.

I have another friend, Laura, who says just going to a Catholic girls school can turn you gay. She also says if you're not married by a certain age, you become a "spinster," which is one of several euphemisms (vocab word!) for lesbian.

What do you think, Mary Richards? I'm desperate to know.

Gratefully yours,

Julie Marie Wade,
Class of 1997,
Agnostic & Democrat

3.

Mary Tyler Moore, Inc.
Culver City, California

January 14, 1999

Dear Mary Tyler Moore:

I'm sending this letter to Mary Tyler Moore, Inc., hoping it will actually
reach you & not just someone sorting through your mail. My mom's friend
found the address when writing to celebrities to request items for a church
auction, & she said you were very kind & sent an autographed copy of the
"Chuckles Bites the Dust" script, which I hear garnered quite a bit of
money for Calvary Lutheran & its related ministries.

This letter isn't a request so much as an expression of gratitude. As it is, I'm
probably too old to be writing fan letters (sophomore in college), but there's
some part of me that just can't seem to resist. You've been my favorite
actress for such a long time, & I feel like I've grown up with you. I started
watching <u>The Dick Van Dyke Show</u> when it debuted on Nick at Nite in
1991, & then <u>The Mary Tyler Moore Show</u> followed the next year, & I was
immediately addicted. I started reading books about you (<u>The Woman
Behind the Smile</u>, etc.) & watching films you've been in—your performance
in <u>Ordinary People</u> is especially good—& I think in a lot of ways, just being
able to focus on something (someone) outside the tiny bubble of my
upbringing has enabled me to grow up & become the questioning & open-
minded nineteen-year-old woman I am today.

I recently ended a relationship with a guy I've had an on-again, off-again romance with since the beginning of freshman year. We fought terribly toward the end, & Ben (that's his name) said something to me that I wanted to dismiss as just sour grapes but that I'm thinking now might have been more true than not. He said my problem is that I don't tailor the relationship to the person I'm with; I already have a pre-set notion of what a relationship should be—I guess a kind of Platonic ideal—& I'm always trying to make the person I like fit into an already-drawn picture. Ben said he felt like I wanted him to play Rob Petrie (play or be, I'm not sure which, or if it would have mattered) so I could play Laura, & we could imitate some version of some TV show that never even existed anyway.

I have to admit I really like the idea of the simple, easy life those characters shared with each other. I mean, it's a far cry from the family in Ordinary People. I like the idea of being someone's beautiful wife & a dancer & giving big, well-attended parties where people entertain each other with songs & comedy routines. It seemed so safe there, but not boring. There were problems of course, but nothing life-threatening or damaging long-term.

Sometimes I think you gave me two portraits of how life could be for a woman: the married life & the single life, & both of them seem like so much fun it's hard not to want to emulate them. When I'm not dating anybody, I tell myself it's better that way because of being with your girlfriends & having that freedom to be open to whoever may come along. I think about the theme song & "love is all around," & everything feels charged with potential. You never know who you might meet or where you might live, & your character is so brave to pack up her car & drive to a big, unfamiliar city, find her own apartment & a job & make friends & hobbies, & I want to do that, too. It scares me a little because I've never lived farther than an hour away from home (in a dormitory, no less), so I haven't really been on my own for real yet, & I'm not 100% sure I <u>can</u> "make it on my own." But I want to try, & Mary Richards motivates me to keep trying to be brave & independent. Next year I am even planning to study abroad.

But then there's Laura Petrie, who I keep coming back to & the possibility of sharing a life with someone. How would that work? I mean, you've been married three times & gone through two divorces. You've had a miscarriage & had your own grown child die. Clearly, your personal experiences are far less ideal than those you've portrayed.

I remember that interview you did with <u>TV Guide</u> (back in 1993, I think), & you said—I underlined it & still keep the quote on my bulletin board—"I'm not so fearful anymore. I've already seen the darkness." But how does that work for you? Are you ever jealous of the women you've played? Do you ever wish your own life had been more like theirs?

Most of the time I feel like I'm being pushed along by this current. It's so strong, & even to go <u>with</u> it I'm always moments away from drowning. To swim against it would be almost impossible. And I don't know where it comes from. My parents, sure, & society at large, & religion & school—they all play a part; they all contribute. I mean, everything seems to be about preparing me for this life I'm going to have, or at least this life I'm <u>supposed</u> to have, & I think it's hard to avoid thinking of that life as anything but an either/or proposition. It's also hard to figure out what I actually want because I'm so aware of what I'm supposed to want & what I'm supposed to feel.

So here's the thing: I get into this mindset where I have to plan, where I have to calculate the future & weigh every risk & consider all the possible outcomes & consequences of every choice, & I don't want to be this big conformist (at least I don't <u>think</u> that's what I want), but I don't know how to avoid being one either. And the problem with shows like <u>The Dick Van Dyke Show</u> & <u>The Mary Tyler Moore Show</u>—as much as I love them—is that they're meant, in a certain way, to be allegorical, right? I mean, Rob Petrie is a kind of Everyman figure, & Mary Richards is a kind of Everywoman figure, & so many people are projecting their fantasies onto these characters that they have to be flexible enough—maybe vacuous enough—to accommodate all those expectations. Which means that, even though they seem original & unique, all television characters (perhaps to varying extents) are conformists of necessity. That's what I'm thinking anyway. That there are no true renegades on television, & maybe none in the real world either.

My parents have accused me of becoming distant. I have gotten quieter in the last few years, & I notice I'm not as confident as I used to be. Maybe it's that girls & gender & math thing, but that can't be the whole explanation. I think it's not so much insecurity as maybe a kind of humility. I feel humbled by how little I actually know, & I feel confused by how I thought I knew more than this. At ten, I thought I had solved all the riddles of the universe, & sometimes I think I must have forgotten things (premature Alzheimer's?) because everything I knew then seemed so real it couldn't have been an illusion. But maybe it was.

Which brings me back to Ben, & I'm just perplexed as to how not to dwell on what you've seen & admired & wanted to be like for so long. Most people want to get married & have kids and live in a nice house with a yard &

plenty of space to move around in, & I don't think that's inherently bad or good, but what is it? Is it conformity? Ben says I'm more creative than that, more imaginative. He says I write over my own experiences with more idyllic versions of what actually occurred. Does that mean I'm a liar? Doesn't everyone do that, to a certain extent? Are we all liars? Why is the truth so hard to find?

Before Ben, I dated this guy named Ari for a few months. I guess he kind of did to me what I did to Ben: tried to program me into his equation for a happy life. He wanted to be a minister (I'm sure he will be), & I'm not so religious anymore, & he wanted to be with someone who would lead the choir or teach Sunday school & never swear or smoke or set a bad example for the congregation in any way. Well, I like to swear sometimes. It's liberating. And I've sampled cigarettes, & I've gotten high a few times, & I don't think it's such a crime. (I certainly don't think it's evil.) And even though I'm probably never going to be a true bad-ass like Rizzo, I'm already way past Sandra Dee. Does that make sense? It's like I just haven't been able to experience so many things, & now I'm hungry (starving, actually) to get out & try everything. I want to see more than Washington, Oregon, and California before I die. And I want to taste some exotic foods & fancy wines & have my own car & get drunk & have sex and spend one night all by myself without being scared.

Ari dumped me because he said he couldn't see himself spending the rest of his life with me & what would be the point of going on dating when the ending was a foregone conclusion? People are already starting to pair off, & I guess I was pushing Ben to pair off with me because some part of me just doesn't believe love can take you by storm. I always expect to have to seek it out & sculpt it a little. Like Amy said in <u>Little Women</u>: "After all, one does have some say as to whom one loves."

Do you think that's true, Ms. Moore? I remember this song from church (it's hard to get all the old religious clutter out from the brain...) about knocking & the door would be opened unto you, but then I heard somewhere else, in a story or a myth of some kind, about knocking & a door shall appear. I like that second idea better. I think in a lot of ways you've been the door other people have knocked on to have it opened for them. You've shown us options for our lives, particularly as women. Laura Petrie wore pants, & it caused a scandal. Mary Richards slept with men she didn't marry. For your time & in your way, you were being radical. I can only hope for my time & in my own way, I will be, too.

Maybe I will even make a door appear that no one else has ever walked through. No guarantees of course, but here's to trying.

Yours truly,

Julie Marie Wade
Ordal Hall #106
Pacific Lutheran University
Tacoma, WA 98447

# ADVENT

"Because it can be neither forgotten nor changed, the past must be redeemed."

—Linda Marie-Gelsomina Zerilli

# ADVENT (YEAGER)

*For Kim & Matt*

What does it mean that tonight
a loggerhead turtle pads softly
onto the starlit South Carolina
shore, planting her eggs—no longer
possessions—in the feeble crosshatch
of uncoverable sand?

(I am waiting in line at the
Piggly Wiggly, three fruits in
each hand, preparing to prepare
sangria for my lover's family.)

Or are we gawking at vines growing
out of a wall—quiet cupola
of crepe myrtle crowning the
Historic Candy Company of
Old Savannah?

Georgia… only a peach tree away.

*

And the not-quite-sister-&-
brother-in-law who live just outside
Atlanta—telling us over
Thai food of their
neighborhood tragedy:
"In Fayetteville, where Evander
Holyfield lives"—because we can't stop, even now,

71

these tangents—
"a girl killed her grandparents when they
forbade her to see the woman she loved."

*Heavenly Creatures* conspicuously absent
from the Fayetteville video store.
"What got me was the grandfather
at the flash of the knife,
trying to run up the stairs…"

How we sigh to the soothe
of coconut milk, rent Margaret Cho's
*Revolution.*

Another suburb, I slip—"swollen with sorrow."

※

Or Greenlake again, with the first
woman I ever gave thought to
loving—how it passed slowly, like a
sailboat riding a signet-ring storm.
Nothing between us now but the
acknowledgment.
"Someday you'll write a poem
about this," & laughs.

But what does she mean?
A poem about the primitive crush,
the existential infatuation?

Or this seabird by our feet—so much
more palpable—whose fresh catch on
closer inspection reveals a
fish hook snared in the craw,
& what we mistook for
pleasure at his head-shaking,
feather-twitching feast announces
itself a bib of darkening blood.

And I tell Becky, who I
haven't seen for three years,
whose countenance is a compass
I can no longer read (but
cherish still in abstraction), "I don't know
what it means to be useless this way."
It's not apathy that holds my hands so close to
my sides, but some strange & sobering resignation.

That is, I know my place, & the bird's
place, & the trenches of language
that divide us. Selfish is another story,
which I understand better than I'd like, the way
this poem quickly shifts from the bird & his plight,
the daughters & their knife, the loggerhead
& her instinctive (is it hope?) for the future—
& becomes about me.

*

"Because you're the poet," Angie will say
when I descend
this plane later today in Denver.

And the implied meaning here
is that birds & turtles & even strangers
in newspaper print & dinner conversation have
their own poems—make them—are them.

I still can't tell you where this poem
begins, chronology
a cause long ago lost on me.
Home is a fault line that
strikes the earth differently
now, ruptures the pen's
smooth line like a polygraph.
*Am I telling the truth?*
*What is the truth?*
*Does it matter?*

*

And then I think of my one
time going under—
that solitary pleasure of sinking backward
into myself.

"Start at a hundred &
count down to zero," the surgeon said.
"Let the numbers fall off as you say them."

99. Who was it broke the sound barrier? What was his name?

96. Did Grandma June sense it that Christmas? Did she realize I wasn't
coming back?

95. Maxwell Smart—no, no, not yet.

92. Such a harsh summer. Even the clouds had run dry.

Slipping off now,

90. And that wreath with all the purple candles, & caroling, &—

\*

The rest of your life… only a peach tree away.

Thomas Kinkade, Painter of Light
*The End of a Perfect Day*

Dear Dad,

I saw a bumper sticker the other
day for Alcoholics Anonymous. I
had forgotten their slogan: "I'm a
friend of Bill W." And the irony
was—how much wished I could be
a friend of Bill W. too.

Online gallery - http://www.thomaskinkade.com

**POSTCARD**

Bill Wade
Boeing Company, 2003

5 years till retirement

# MORTON'S GIRL

Elegant as understatement, she steps before the blue felt board of a false winter. Someone in the studio will attach a few stars. Lights... Cameras...

From their cross-hatch chairs, they admire the mute schoolgirl from southern San Fran whose mother has auctioned her fragile face for the selling of Christendom's oldest concoction.

Before this, pistachio pudding & angel hair pasta. Snap. Preliminary photograph. "Yes, that's lovely," twirling her yellow umbrella.

Someone in the studio has hung the moon up crooked. CUT!

"Just pretend you're walking on water, splash in a puddle or two." The squeak of galoshes an afterthought.

"Good, now pretend that you're singing." Flash. Snap. Long past her bedtime. "Just like a musical—just like you're singin' in the rain."

## MR. CLEAN

Middle age lumbers on—a big yellow dog—
haggard nafs; mirage of the Fortune Five Hundred
-----------------------------------------------------
Late night lifting at the 24-Hour Fitness Club:
I see a man, strapping,
Paul Bunyan resurrected
with a dark cheek & a streak of
sweat tracing the line of bilateral symmetry
down his body
solar plexus personified

What we don't tell our mothers...

About the L.A. Connection & the last "nice girl"
who was your lover's second cousin
twice removed
-----------------------------------------------------
I never stay long at parties unless
a producer's around,      a couple of porn flicks in
my younger days before steroids bought
stamina & fucking turned
futile again
-----------------------------------------------------
So when the job & it's not your dream but so what?
You're a homo from Ohio—not Vin Diesel
(not bad either)

At least it'll keep you in currency till the next "big break" breaks over
your head & the Joe Montana dreams resurface
Touchdown! Touchdown! just waiting for someone to score

*How you always want to touch him when you're down...*
------------------------------------------------------------
Now the barber shaves your head clean again, no more peach fuzz,
& smiles beside your naked scalp

[Flex.] [Flush.] [Flex.] [Flush.]

Fuck that Brawny paper towel man they think is so robust!

With any luck, you'll meet a nice suburban wife—sweet talk & small:
"What? No girlfriend waiting in the wings?"
Shake your head, sigh; decide (this once) to let her buy you dinner

## "This Thing I Want, I Know Not What"

(A Correspondence with Mick Kelly—

the strange, gifted, & lonely protagonist of

*The Heart is a Lonely Hunter*)

Because I've been there before, at the river's edge,
with my damp trousers cuffed around my ankles.
And there's no one watching, but there always is,
when you descend naked as the water.

*This was a very fine and secret place. Close around were thick cedars so that she was completely hidden by herself. The radio was no good tonight—somebody sang popular songs that all ended in the same way. It was like she was empty.*

*

When I said it then, I meant to lie;
I meant to lie & singe my mother's eyes.
But what if no one could, & what if no one would
ever think of asking for my hand in marriage?

*This would be the first party she had ever given. She had never even been to more than four or five. Last summer she had gone to a prom party. But none of the boys asked her to prom or dance, she just stood by the punch bowl until all the refreshments were gone and then went home.*

Difference is the darkest word in this whole
hard language; queer is what they
call you when you won't fit in your box.
At best: invisible; at worst: ambiguous.

*The radio and the lights in the house were turned off. The night was very dark. Suddenly Mick began hitting her thigh with her fists. She pounded the same muscle with all her strength until the tears came down her face. But she could not feel this hard enough. The rocks under the bush were sharp. She grabbed a handful of them and began scraping them up and down on the same spot until her hand was bloody. Then she fell back to the ground and lay looking up at the night. With the fiery hurt in her leg she felt better. She was limp on the wet grass, and after a while her breath came slow and easy again.*

✻

Under the pelt of his skin, I was hiding. I still
remember how heavy he was, rocking
from side to side. I didn't want to be that kind of woman,
the kind that turns to sawdust in their hands.

*They both turned at the same time. They were close against each other. She felt him trembling and her fists were tight enough to crack. "Oh, God," he kept saying over and over. It was like her head was broke off from her body and thrown away. And her eyes looked up straight into the blinding sun while she counted something in her mind. And then this was the way. This was how it was.*

*

So when I say it now, I mean it; I have gone
back & redeemed the lie: I cannot marry, man or otherwise.
But in my heels, a hard lump I am rolling, a wish
for absolution: instead of a callus, a parting kiss.

*Why hadn't the explorers known by looking at the sky that the world was round? The sky was
curved, like the inside of a huge glass ball, very dark blue with the sprinkles of bright stars. The
night was quiet. There was the smell of warm cedars. She was not trying to think of the music
at all when it came back to her.*

*

And you know too, when the floorboards creak,
& the shadows call, how silence looms—
deft & instrumental, like a striking cloud—
how silence breaks, your once-&-only ally.

*She listened in a quiet, slow way and thought the notes out like a problem in geometry so she
would remember. She could see the shape of the sounds very clear and she would not forget them.*

*

So this is the symphony then, this the sorrow.

# Bridges (Or a Letter to a Woman I Once Loved)

Dear K—

*on your 26th birthday*

[Why is it, with all this water under the bridge, we still can't stop it from burning?]

I will be generous with you, this once, as pertains to your little green book, your first volume. I have read it all, & with a lump forming in my throat that even this coffee, for all its virtues, has not washed down. Has failed to drown.

And we know about failure, don't we? About writing & being written over. Out.

Once, we were novel. Like the pages. Fresh & full of promise. Our ink was hardly dry.... But what was it your teacher told you about the long draft? Difficulty, was it, sustaining character? Chapters interfered with your momentum, slit the throat of plot.

For my part, a poem isn't a novel either, but I was thinking epic when I first undressed with you, backs turned to quiet corners, eyes unerringly closed: my more-than-sister who gave me Sappho & Cisneros, who sobbed into sleep in my arms.

And we are full of surprises, aren't we?

Your early marriage to Certainty, my reappraisal: "Just because she's jumping off a bridge doesn't mean I have to..."

It's snowing here in Pittsburgh. That's a letter-writing kind of thing to say. And true. It's a cold March we're having, & Angie's waiting in the car, warming the engine. Convenient now—to say a woman came between us, when it was your fear (& later, my unforgiveness) that finally broke us, like dark river water, in our fall.

Of the stories, I can say they were "efficient," "effective," even "eloquent" in places where a guard was let down. (Gently, I hope, for his sake.) And a good length, all of them. Not a single stroke too long.

K, hear me now: blessing your life I am no longer a part of. Our ending too abrupt, though lacking nothing where intensity was concerned.

You said it yourself once, when you were still a poet, that springboard you left for the sea: "It's not practical, the absence of paragraphs, all that dreadful white space just demanding…"

Here in the snow, I write your name & watch the sky erase it. And then, being only a poet & lost for words, do all that I can do. Quietly.

Caesura.

Pause.

# Thinking of Carl Lull, His Deaf Mother, His Left Hand

This will be a bloody, beautiful poem.

This will be my tribute to you,
Carl Lull, & to your name—with its perfect consonance,
as if a literary character I'd created.

But it wasn't me who invented you.  It was
your mother, a train whistle of a woman
who shaped words with her hands, & your father,
who bent over the massive steering wheel of a Metro bus & drove it
long after sundown into the vacant squares of the city.

They had been expecting you, eager & fearful, wondering
whether your ears would be open like bright café windows, or closed
like a vessel of sand.

And you came, & you heard, but you did not conquer.
It was not your ears, but your right fist closed, deadened,
with the left one reaching all around.
Your mother, perhaps because she had been different all her life
& knew the weariness of the world's crossed eyes,
snatched the pencil from your young south paw, your agile, itching fingers.

"No writing with that hand!" your father bellowed,
& little-boy you blushed & quivered.

The left hand, you learned, was for watches & wedding bands,
but not for playing baseball or scrawling the alphabet.

And here's where the poem does something tricky, advances

a solid ten years to where you & I are standing together
in Language Arts class—mine the cautious cursive, yours the indecipherable
sprawl.

"You write like a monster," I said, words I've always wished to rescind.
But you, Carl Lull, looked me sharp in the eyes, remained unshaken:
"So what? You run like a girl."

Still today I'm stunned by your rebound.
And the fact you became a track star
only adds to the irony.

All those years of elementary school I had been thinking how
strange you were—
your mother who couldn't hear the smashed glass
from a stray baseball but who could articulate wild
operas of words with only the curve of her hands.

It didn't make sense you heard everything,
even the harsh stories other students told behind your back.

As if you were always there...
As if you were always listening...

Yet your own page so appalling—
your right hand awkward as a crane,
your left, quiet as if crippled,
as if contained by an invisible cast
that no one had been asked to sign.

I cut the picture of you from the college paper & posted it up on my wall.
Not because I loved you—though in a way I did—but because then, as now,
I wanted to remember about beginnings.

I don't know if you're using the left hand again, or if you have a child
perhaps, who reaches for a pen with hers.

All grown-up now, alumnae
from a former life but bearing still
remnants of its burns & fetters.

And I say, bless you, Carl Lull—a lefty at heart—
from a right-handed poet with some lessons to learn
about the marginal space & the 10% place &
the rest of her implacable life.

## PROPHET (POSSIBLY)

For Bryan O'Leary, who, at ten, may be the best man to begin marching. *Where?* We're not sure yet, but everyone seems to agree marching is necessary. In times like these, an inventor will lead them; a small, preliterate visionary. Maybe there is some hope for the world after all. Maybe a small face unfurrowed & a crew cut with one dangling curl. That's our poster child: third round of the Revolution. High knees. Dirty khakis. A mother who can't read much better, but he can see—thick mesh-net of blue-black lashes, & a natural pause. *Caesura.* (I make it a point never to write about children.) Pink eraser ground down to the stem. "Just 'cause I can't read it doesn't mean I don't know what it says." I study his eyes. (Point taken.)

## FENTON GLEN

So death isn't really about the dying.... But I didn't know, back in 1990 when Rick Brown was hanging from a tree behind the Fauntleroy Community Church overlooking the creek & the little stone bench scattered with cherry blossoms, which was the closest we came to a Lover's Lane in the dreamscape called Fauntlee Hills.

I had been to Fenton Glen a number of times, but always & only with my father. He didn't want me wandering there alone at night, or out with my friends on one of our ill-fated picnics.

*What could possibly have happened to us?* I wondered, there in the vice-grip of the virtuous suburbs, where every window left a lamp lit & police patrolled in search of unlocked cars or a lost cat rummaging through overturned trash.

"Bad things happen everywhere," he grimaced, tightening his hold. "The world isn't what it used to be, that's for certain."

I have a hard time imagining what my father recalls, when all this Mike Brady brick was such a blessing.... But I knew Rick Brown, of course I knew Rick Brown, from the late nights listening to the parent talk, he & Judy tag-teaming Linda & Bill at Rack-O.

"He cheats, you know," my mother whispered to me when I appeared in the doorway holding a tray of bologna & cream cheese roll-ups. "Watch him sometime, you'll see. He switches the cards when he thinks nobody's looking."

And that was the first of his fatal mistakes, for my mother was *always* looking.

I was there in the house the day Judy Brown confessed over Tetley tea that she had never loved her husband, only married him for the diamond he flashed her way & the fear she couldn't trump him if she tried. "There was nobody better," she sighed.

They had two children & a Scottie dog, & the diamond squeezed tight on her manicured finger, so she took it off & stowed it away in a safety deposit at Seafirst.

No one was home when the papers came, but a man in a too-short blue suit stood on the porch & waited. Rick didn't even suspect until he pulled in the drive & was handed his elegy, sealed in sleek manila.

"You knew," I said, accusing my mother.
"Julie Marie, come now, away from that window…"

So death isn't really about the dying, not even when Scottie is first to go. She had him "put down." I didn't even know he was sick… my mother slapped my face when I said it—"the way she put down their father."

She sued him for everything, the house & the car; she stowed her children away at her mother's. And Rick said, broken at last, "All right then, you win, no contest."

It was spring, my own father away on business. I knew the rules, no walking in the park alone. And Judy came by the house to tell my mother, "I got him—no strings attached!" on her hurried way to meet Rick at the Glen.

There were cherry trees spilling their seasonal bliss, & Judy with her high heels sharpening on pavement. She walked down to the site of their settlement, behind the church where they had been, for many years, such faithful members.

And even though I wasn't there, I knew how the scene looked, how the sirens screeched & wailed past my bedroom window, & the note he had gingerly pinned to his tie for some gloved hand to loosen, then let down...

We all let each other down by dying, but Rick wanted her to read his message in the thick noose & the slender throat of the tree. "YOU DID THIS TO ME," in black ball-point pen, the kind my father carried in his pocket. And maybe she was sorry, or maybe she was glad, but I ached that way when a carousel spins around too hard.

Because I knew then that no one was safe, that my father was right, that death was remorse & revenge. He just plain strung himself up & hung himself out there to dry.

Bad things can happen anywhere

*Fenton Glen, my young boyfriend aimless under my blouse...*

The world isn't what it used to be

*The high branches, growing back from where they had snapped...*

Rick Brown, beyond us all now, no longer cheating at Rack-O.

Saturdays I still think of him mowing his lawn, with a manual no less, when everyone else had gone electric...

Then off in the distance, I hear her voice: *Julie Marie, come away from that window!*

# EPIPHANY

"I have discarded clarity as worthless. Working in darkness, I have discovered lightning."

—André Breton

## EPIPHANY

What they told you to look for at the end of the poem—simulacrum (at least) of resolution. Is there a place for lamentation? catharsis?

We have entered the epoch of lowercases where Truth tips over its hat & God gurgles down like a rumor of indigestion.

Let me not suggest infinity, lopsided 8 floating in ether. Let me not suggest quarrel or victuals, which (being old words) are subject to breakage.

Did you ever make a diorama? Perhaps from a shoebox & in the third grade?

I am not sure if the question mark goes inside the quotation mark—always, sometimes, or never.

Introducing the Great Mysteries of our time. If there is after-thought, what shall we call this: mind sharpening its knife for inaugural incision?

Give up on interjections, friend; they only slow you down. Confess to your good nature that truth (like a wizened troll) clings only to verbs, to actions.

We regress to diagramming sentences again. Imagine: if the whole were the sum of its parts, I could love algebra without the fear of fractions.

Not like revelation, which happens over time—which lingers. But a voice in the head like a natural heart: insistent as a kiss, & just as sudden.

Oh, Chester! Cold winters I can't bear to think what we did before you. I only suppose we carried on as women have—for centuries—inventing anonymously what men continue taking the credit for.

But that's me, in this life, being cynical, & for that I'm sorry, Chester, I really am.

I think we could have meant something to each other in another life, or that perhaps we did already in the immaculate hindsight (or is it foresight?) called reincarnation.

I might have even loved you, Chester, freezing to flush on the ice floes of Farmington, Maine. Might have remembered you as Erich Neupert from my new life's grammar school, who wore gray corduroy pants with gaping zippers & whose mother had his hair buzzed a little too close to his melon-like head & who—this is the part that's relevant—loved to ice skate & couldn't care a wit that other boys called him queer.

Once, I went to his house & saw his collection of Care Bears spread out neatly on his bed, & his sister Shavon who hardly said a word but who, like Erich, had light freckles & was always glowing around her temples just enough to believe there might have actually been a light bulb beaming inside her brain.

But this is our story, Chester, I almost forgot, & Erich Neupert did not drop out of grammar school, nor—to my knowledge—go on to make a name for himself as an ear-warming entrepreneur.

What if I had been there that day? You at fifteen, a gladiolus stem of a boy set to swaying, spinning on the toe of your white leather shoe as if no one was watching—forgetting me, forgetting everyone around us on the elegant pond, & unlike George Bailey & his brother in the fictional fast-forward, there was no soft spot in the firm water, so you did not break through, but your ears were cold & pinkening in the ferocious air, & the inventor inside you insisted on wire & wool to accommodate the chill. Your grandmother could sew, & so, & so...Women again, at the bidding of men, & soon this new commodity of yours was on the market.

I imagine on an eight-degree morning in Pittsburgh, PA, how it might have felt to figure-eight my way into your fairy tale; how you might have twirled me in the gray-corduroy cold & placed your mittened hands over my ears, promising something more permanent in the future. We might have stumbled into a snow bank together, laid down here at this intersection in snow-angel country, flapping our arms wildly on the luminous ground with warm flaps pulled over our ears & the sound of our laughter rising, anonymous in the air.

Chester Greenwood, I can see it so clearly now: how I'd be the girl you'd always forget to remember when Farmington became "Ear Muff Capital of the World" & December 21 dedicated 'specially to your honor. I'd think of you, the boy I kissed during a cold spell in another life, & light with my lover's match—& lambskin covering my ears—a candle for you—for this & every other Christmas.

# Vanna's Dream

Morning's oyster gleam, & a star rising over North Carolina. Cheer season & sixteen again. When the words were hers, she still believed they mattered. The light slipping in soft now between the curtains. A boy she kissed & stayed the night with is now long gone. But there was heat in his body given over to her—like a blessing, like the Holy Ghost taken on human form. *Go team! Go team!* And oh, how she dreams of the sidelines! Looking pretty, her mama said, was the best revenge; they have to hate you a little while 'fore they love you.

*2, 4, 6, 8, Who do we appreciate?* The lions, the tigers, the bears... Her skirt flounces up in the air, but the briefs are there, which is good, which is safety & modesty for a PG-13 kind of girl with thin blond hair & a Bible epigraphed by Jesus. "And the Word became flesh," & the boy became distant, & the cheer squad limped along to the semi-finals. She knew the words then, like a glossy coat of paint across her tongue. She knew how to smile when they threw her higher than she liked, how to kick & curtsy, clap & count back to the next song.

When the angel came to her in a dream, Vanna wondered what did he mean in the future—"Every night will be prom night" & crisp dollar bills.

"The word is in you," the angel said. "And you will reveal it, letter by letter."

# Breaking Out (Or a Letter to Brandith Irwin)

It's hard to tell who I hated more: you, or me, or my acne. Was it my blistering red pores or your bold face—smooth as untouched snow—peering down at me over over-sized, black glasses?

At eleven, nobody understands what's happening to her body: only the way it can betray so entirely the last trusted expectation that a face is still a face & not a mine field.

My mother was not ready for ring-side seats at the oil well of my complexion. I was not ready for the astringent's sting after half another hour between her tweezers.

"The meanness," she said. "It's the *meanness* coming out of you."

I must have been a pretty mean kid, Dr. Irwin. Even in fifth grade, volcanoes oozing from my skin, & my mother's sharp nails digging in, digging deep down in, & then in summertime how the contagion spread like a shawl sprawling over my shoulders, like a colony of red soldiers drumming the bumpy trail of spine.

And she would straddle me each night after dinner, pinning my hands behind my back or over my head, tangled up in the trellis hanging over the bed, until the pus & the blood rose up from the white heads & the black heads & my mother said, "Look, it's the meanness coming out of you, I never had a pimple a day in my life, but your father sure did," & there's something about that kind of inheritance that makes you want to slit your own throat before it's swimsuit season again & Laura Wissing's little brother says, "What's wrong with your skin? Why is it so red?"

*Because I'm mean, little boy. Watch out for me. I'm a witch in a candy-covered cottage.*

But Brandith Irwin, I'm not finished with you yet. You're not getting off the hook so easy. At least with Rose Kennedy, there was some gentleness as her talcum hand slid into its glove, some softness in her face till she tilted back the mirror. Do you remember the note my mother made me send? It was a ransom— my life in exchange for the apology I rendered.

"Dear Dr. Kennedy... Dear Dr. Lawrence... Dear Dr. Rosenthal... " I saw so many of them, but you were the dermatologist I most despised.

*Dear Dr. Irwin,*

*I'm sorry I behaved badly in your office today. I didn't mean it. I am going through a sensitive time concerning my skin right now, & sometimes it causes me to take out my frustrations on the wrong person.*

*Sincerely,*
*Julie Marie Wade*

Here's my retraction: I didn't mean a word of it. I think today as I thought then how cold you were, how cruel, to a little girl with a bad permanent & the first stabs of mascara flecking her eyes. And I hope somewhere you're reading this note & that you're embarrassed, Brandith Irwin, for the time you held my chin in your hand & determined that with "another round of Accutane" & "perhaps some minor cosmetic surgery" equivalent to spackling—*we can graft the skin from somewhere else & fill her stretched pores in*—I could possibly become in my hypothetical life some version of "a slightly pretty girl."

So this is the meanness coming out of me, as predicted.

If I had a voodoo doll & I believed in that sort of thing, I'd pock every pore in your smug countenance, rising out of the ash of your white-gray skin, until you were hard-pressed at your own mirror to puncture every one of them; abate the burn with powder. Still, the little ant-hills, & your patients looking at you funny, & your credibility dwindling with every oil rig that spilled its precious cargo.

I'd wish you a lonely girl in West Seattle with a long bridge between you & the city, with a stone-rough road between you & the rest of the world, & I'd wish me the one to sit in judgment over you in a lab coat & a visor with a miner's light & all the framed diplomas on the wall of my corner office with a view of ferry docks & downtown traffic, & I'd shake my head, consult the charts, & tell you that with a little luck & a lot of prayer you might just become "bearable to look at." Then, snapping my glove & brandishing the bright lamp on the overhead table, I'd smile & say, "Someday you might even be a slightly pretty girl…

Once we get the meanness out of you—that is."

*The False Mirror*

Artist: Rene Magritte

1928, Oil on Canvas, 54 x 80.9 cm

Museum of Modern Art, New York

*As a love poem*

You are my looking glass, my lachrymatory.
Tears rush out to you like oceans of sky.

Cumulus, for comfort: each pillow of possible.
Pupil, a vintage record, still revolves.

Sleep I want to sweep from your eyes.
Dreams spilling forth from a delicate spindle.

These tacit understandings, like syllables mounting a tongue—
Reflex of blink, of swallow.

Or that blindness in love, known best as hallucination:
Empathy dressed down as mannequin inside the old macabre of Macy's.

To see & believe we are known, in color as in monochrome—
In rods as in cones.

When you are vulnerable, we'll say retina, meaning sensitive.
When you are witty, we'll say vitreous, for humor.

These tacit understandings, like a loosened lash—
A lost wish released into the cosmos.

When you close them, watch for portraits on the under-lid:
Cool-skinned girls cantering through marshes.

I am your looking glass, your lachrymatory.
Put thou thy tears in my bottle!

Because what I wanted more than anything was not to be the only child & not the one on whom everything was riding for my parents & my grandmother & my aunt who was also godmother—a whole family of fledglings desperate for a swan. And because my father had been a traveling salesman like his father before him, & when he gave it up to spend more time with his family, I always felt somehow that we had let him down. Or *I* had, by not being a boy or by being more studious than adventurous & not liking fishing or golfing or sailing or ever even caring to learn. How when I turned vegetarian at nineteen for a four-month stint I thought I had broken his heart but really it was already broken from years before when I didn't invite him to my piano recital & got embarrassed when he cheered too loud at the cross-country race & because I didn't think at the bottom line he was smart enough to have done all the things he wanted to do with his life, & he thought about me that I was "too smart for my own good."

Once a year on Family Fun Nite we tucked it all inside us like cold hands rolled up within the interminable sleeves of Woolrich sweaters, & though there were no brothers & sisters, we piled into the car like a big, happy family, & my mother had people she could talk to while my father & I wandered over to the miniature golf & the fishing game where the person on the other side of the partition puts something perfectly beautiful & unexpected on the end of your line, like a slinky or a glow-in-the-dark yo-yo or any number of edible treats like poppy cock or peanut brittle, & so in a way we were fishing & golfing together after all, & my selfishness & his submissiveness were no longer under scrutiny the way they were when we became divided by my mother, & since this was long before I knew how the story would end, I could just keep imagining that my father would always be my friend, & that Saturdays at Winchell's Donuts wouldn't be forsaken for preoccupation with my waistline & disillusionment with the lack of same-aged friends.

We'd run into my mother again at the cakewalk, where she would man the baking table & contribute her own version of a pineapple upside down cake or a tinker cake with two-inch chocolate icing. And it didn't matter that it didn't taste good. What I wanted was a chance to win, & dancing to the music on the masking-taped squares, & hoping that the one stop would be me in the Russian roulette of pastries, & then I'd get to pick whichever cake whoever's mother made was going home with me, & it wouldn't be the tinker cake but someone else's raspberry lemon with cream cheese frosting & the cellophane coverall sunken at the center, just begging to be peeled off.... Some years I went home with three cakes from playing so long, & my father carried them out to the car in a box top he'd borrowed from someone, & my mother said her good-byes to the militant members of the West Seattle Christian PTA, & I waved to the kids I never talked to in school but who somehow, after dark, became less sinister & more believable as friends.

As rode home, I sagged into sleep in the back seat between my boxes of cakes & my fishing pole prize & under my father's hand who used to cover six states "from Idaho all the way to Indiana." I never worried about him falling asleep at the wheel or about the future, which was so far ahead you couldn't even see it through the Friday night condensation on the glass, & the empty streets glossy with puddles steeped in lamplight, or the way everything ends abruptly with the red fire-fingers of the dawn.

All of it a dream from which you suddenly wake up.

Gwyneth Paltrow & Blythe Danner
Vancouver, British Columbia
Photographed by Annie Leibovitz

POSTCARD

Today I know less of you than the
day I was born:

Do you miss me?                                    Mother
Have you stopped crying?
Is the lying easier now?                          Fauntlee Hills
                                                  (The Water-View Side)

Please tell me:                                   Eleven years later
Where is my childhood? (Did it
"keep"?)
Do you think you could send it to
me?

Barnes & Noble - Waterworks

## Obituary for Robert Miller,
## Whose Absence Is Felt Again Today

In April 1992, Robert Miller of Seattle, WA, aged 69, died of complications from cancer. He was survived by his long-time friend & roommate, Maestro David Kyle.

Today I can see not even his kind face clearly, but I remember the garnet ring he wore on the fourth finger of his speckled hand—how round & dark it was, how clearly not "costume." My mother had many rings, but none like Robert's. He was the first man I ever knew who wore a ring neither wedding band nor high school souvenir. I noticed too that when I sat up on his ample lap to admire the jewel, my father always lurched a little, as if wishing I would keep my distance, as if wanting to pull me away.

My parents met Robert in the late Eighties when they became part of a fortuitous theatre group that Robert had commissioned with his sizeable pocketbook & passionate commitment to the arts. He was a short, thick man, bald & distinguished, with fingers quietly conducting each score. He wore fine Armani suits (the name he taught me) & shoes he had shined bright as businessmen's at the airport.

It was strange, I thought, for all his style, that he paid these tense, pretentious people to play his friends. Each week Robert sent a fresh batch of tickets to each favored suburban home, their assortment wide & compelling as choco-lates: this week the symphony, next the ballet, two Sundays from now a British farce. And *Madame Butterfly*. And *Miss Saigon*. And every now & then, something lighter—"for the children."

There were five families in his entourage, & he never asked a penny in return. But he didn't drive, so he would have to be chauffeured, & he brought his own cassette along for the ride: soundtrack or classical score. The tickets were always front row or box seats, the best accommodations each venue had to offer. And he preferred the aisle, clapped loud & hard, & sometimes roused himself in spontaneous ovation.

"Is Robert married?" I asked my mom, as we prepared a plate of cookies in his honor. Like Santa Claus, he required this minor compensation—that afterwards he be taken in & fed.

"No," she said & went on about her baking.

"Was he ever?" I pressed, & she shook her head.

"Does he live all alone in that big, old house on Alki?"

And the story went that Robert had a friend who was quite famous in those parts, the reclusive & much-sought-after Maestro David Kyle. Robert never mentioned him in the company of friends, but I heard them talking after, assembled in the drive, when someone's well-trained husband had left to take him home.

"I wonder what the Maestro thinks about us…"

"I'm just relieved we've never had to meet him…"

"Surely they've settled down some since their younger days…"

"Kate-lynn's friend has a voice lesson there next Wednesday."

I never saw behind the ivy on that house, with its stone chimney stolidly puffing. I ate raspberry dribble cake at Mrs. Parker's house when Robert remarked it was the finest he'd ever tasted.

"Who does Mary Parker think she is? Trying to show me up that way!"

Was he lonely, & did the Maestro mind that he was out so often with us all, paying for valet parking?

And when I asked, that one time, refilling his cup: *Why don't you bring your friend with you sometime?*

His eyes snapped open as he reclined in the chair, a pillow buttressing his lower torso. "And which friend is that, pray tell? I have gathered a great many of them at my age."

"The one you live with," I stammered at first—"the man who gives the music lessons."

Knowingly now, propping his feet on the leopard-print ottoman: "Ah, David," with a light in his eye. "He's the secret I'm keeping all to myself."

When Robert died, my parents didn't take me to the funeral. I asked to go, but they were afraid of how it might "scar" me, afraid of what I might hear. My father, knotting his tie in the bedroom mirror: "Do you think there'll be a lot of them there?" And my mother, brushing her hair, daubing her ears with perfume—the way I used to love to watch her: "They're artists, for Christ's sake. What would you expect?" Then whisking me out through the door...

If I knew where he was buried, I'd bring a rose to his grave. Garnet-red, well-suited for a boutonnière. I'd tell him how I knew the truth & wasn't afraid, even though there were always grown-up hands covering my ears. I would tell him how I understand the euphemisms better than I'd like, how eyes turn down & voices too, as if they're only doing you a favor.

And I'd remember to him that big, old house shuttered with curtains of green. To the best of my knowledge, the Maestro's still there, & when I'm in town—which isn't often these days— I drive past, with my Secret, smiling.

"To put it in the simplest of terms, I walked away from you. But this time, it wasn't the hardest thing I ever had to do. It was pretty easy, quite honestly, to move, breathe, & speak so freely."

—Nick Alan
Kiva Han Coffee Shop
South Craig Street
Pittsburgh, Pennsylvania

# Personal Acknowledgments

The idea for *Postage Due* came about in the autumn of 2003 when my partner Angie & I were wandering around Squirrel Hill, our first neighborhood in our newly adopted city of Pittsburgh. We had moved to the City of Bridges so I could attend the Master of Fine Arts program at the University of Pittsburgh, & when I graduated in the spring of 2006, I defended a much longer version—close to 150 pages, if memory serves—of the manuscript you find before you now. *Postage Due* became not only my attempt at redeeming an unforgettable & unchangeable past but also an unexpected homage to a city I came, slowly but certainly, to love.

I am thankful for my professors, colleagues, employers, & friends at the University of Pittsburgh, Chatham University, Carnegie Mellon University, and Carlow University. In particular, I want to thank Fatin Abdal-Sabur, Mark Lynn Anderson, Connie Angermeier, Wändi Bruine de Bruin, the late Robyn Dawes, Toi Derricotte, the late Bruce Dobler, Lucy Fischer, Kathryn Flannery, Robin Godfrey, Katie Hogan, Mandy Holbrook, Neepa Majumdar, John Miller, the late Bob Parker, Lisa Parker, Amy Patterson, Kerry Reynolds, Mary Schafer, Pat Schaller, Sarah Scholl, Tracy K. Smith, Helena Studer, Stacey Waite, Gabe Yu, & the Department of Social & Decision Sciences at Carnegie Mellon, an extraordinary place to learn & grow.

I remain indebted always to Nickole Brown & Robert Alexander for selecting this book for the Marie Alexander Poetry Series & for their enthusiastic support of my work. Likewise to Dennis Maloney for guiding this book to print. I am also profoundly grateful for the blurbs provided by four poets whose work I have long admired: Rick Barot, Denise Duhamel, James Allen Hall, & Dawn Lundy Martin. Thank you for taking the time to read my words & offer yours in response.

Praise for the teachers, in perpetuity: Annette Allen, Bruce Beasley, Pamela Beattie, Kathe Curran, Carolyn Du Pen, Cate Fosl, Paul Griner, Sister Janice Holkup, Holly Holland, Beth Kraig, Patsy Maloney, Brenda Miller, Christine Moon, Charles Mudede, Sally McLaughlin, Suzanne Paola, Sister Rosemary Perisich, Donna Qualley, Star Rush, Susan Schroeder, David Seal, Bill Smith, Barbara Temple-Thurston, & Steve VanderStaay.

And for the friends, old & new: Rev Culver, April Davis, Ben Dobyns, Becky Farrell, Dustin Hall, Jason Hanson, Monica Krupinski, Kara Larson, James Leary, Jess Leary, Keely Lewis, Anna Murray, Sara Northerner, Vanessa Ortblad, Elijah Pritchett, Maggie Santolla, Catherine Schaffner, Breeayn Schwanke, Carol Stewart, Jen Thonney, Amy Tudor, & Steve Watkins.

For Kim & Matt Striegel, my incomparable "outlaws," niece Evie, & nephew Nolan ("Hondo"): love, joy, & gratitude.

For Tom Campbell, Dana Anderson, Anna Rhodes, & James Allen Hall, the four points of the compass. Love, joy, & gratitude to you.

For Angie Griffin, the brightest light.

## Literary Acknowledgments

I am grateful to the extraordinary writers whose work appears, excerpted, as section breaks or within the poems themselves: Naomi Shihab Nye (*Red Suitcase*, 1994); Rae Armantrout (*Up to Speed*, 2004); Louise Glück (*The Wild Iris*, 1991); L. Frank Baum (*The Wonderful Wizard of Oz*, 1900); Linda Marie-Gelsomina Zerilli (*Feminism and the Abyss of Freedom*, 2005); Carson McCullers (*The Heart is a Lonely Hunter*, 1940); and André Breton (*What is Surrealism?: Selected Writings*, Franklin Rosemont, ed., 1969).

Put a fresh roach in Jimi's mouth
for me.
Dust off his shoes.
Tell him I wasn't the last time we
met,
but I am "experienced" now.

**POSTCARD**

Emerald City

c/o Spooky Robert at
the Laughing Buddha

219 Broadway Avenue
Capitol Hill, 98102

Born in Seattle in 1979, Julie Marie Wade completed a Master of Arts in English at Western Washington University in 2003, a Master of Fine Arts in Poetry at the University of Pittsburgh in 2006, and a Ph.D. in Humanities with creative dissertation at the University of Louisville in 2012. She is the author of the poetry chapbook *Without* (Finishing Line Press, 2010) and two collections of lyric nonfiction, *Wishbone: A Memoir in Fractures* (Colgate University Press, 2010) and *Small Fires* (Sarabande Books, 2011). Julie lives with her partner and their two cats in the Sunshine State, where she teaches creative writing at Florida International University in Miami.

# THE MARIE ALEXANDER POETRY SERIES

Founded in 1996 by Robert Alexander, the Marie Alexander Poetry Series is dedicated to promoting the appreciation, enjoyment, and understanding of American prose poetry. Currently an imprint of White Pine Press, the series publishes one to two books annually. These are typically single-author collections of short prose pieces, sometimes interwoven with lineated sections, and an occasional anthology demonstrating the historical or international context within which American poetry exists. It is our mission to publish the very best contemporary prose poetry and to carry the rich tradition of this hybrid form on into the 21st century.

Series Editor: Robert Alexander
Editor: Nickole Brown

Volume 16
*Family Portrait: American Prose Poetry 1900–1950*
Edited by Robert Alexander

Volume 15
*All of Us*
Elisabeth Frost

Volume 14
*Angles of Approach*
Holly Iglesias

Volume 13
*Pretty*
Kim Chinquee